FASCINATING PARIS

Texts **Marc Lemonier**   Photographs **Jacques Lebar**

FASCINATING

PARIS

English adaptation by **David W. Cox**

PARIGRAMME

In Paris...

Have the beauty and charm of Paris been sufficiently sung? *"It is no city, it is a world,"* marveled one Renaissance admirer. Indeed. And each succeeding generation has endeavored to discover the multiple facets and layers of this ancient city. Founded on the banks of the Seine, the city has the charms of a port. Capital of a kingdom then a nation, it has the palaces, the avenues and the splendors. A metropolis devouring surrounding countryside, and yet, it has managed to conserve a few village squares within its periphery. A stroll through the capital is also a walk through history. Explorers of the city will be intrigued equally by its aristocratic quarters and humble lanes. Lovers of the city never tire of the sights: the nobility of a monument, the harmony of a street, the refreshing air in a garden, the exhilaration of slipping through a half-open carriage door to discover the greenery in a hidden courtyard. Such fleeting pleasures must be seized instantly. One gaze at the gray slate roofs, at the beige stone façades, and these colors are forever engraved in our souls. A ray of sunshine, unexpectedly glancing off a gurgling fountain, or sparkling on a gilded statue, can make the instant rich and unique. Is the spell broken with the hubbub of outdoor markets, the rumble of traffic, or a few echoes of music drifting from seemingly out of nowhere? Certainly not. The unceasing and omnipresent hum of this thriving, vibrant city – no mere décor – only adds to the intense pleasure of simply being here. In Paris.

The great rose window, western façade.

The Chimera Gallery.

Portal of the Judgment (details).

ΝΟΤRe-Dame De PaRIS

How long does it take to erect a masterpiece? In 1160, Maurice de Sully, Bishop of Paris, decided to construct a new church on Île de la Cité to replace several buildings of lesser importance. The first phase of construction took roughly twenty years. In 1182, the choir was completed and the altar was consecrated. Next, work began on the double-side aisle, and the bays of the nave were erected little by little.

It was 1220 before master sculptors completed the splendid rose window, and 1240 when the two western towers began to rise into the Paris sky.

The 13th-century construction work became more complex as architectural tastes evolved. New bishops modified the orders given to builders Jean and Pierre de Chelles, Jean Ravy, and Raymond du Temple. Windows had to be enlarged. Walls had to rise even higher. At last, Notre Dame Cathedral was completed. People of that time were well aware that the heart of Paris had a masterpiece in a style which only later would be termed Gothic.

How long did it take to mutilate a masterpiece? Only a few centuries later, the job was done by a brief whirlwind of passion during the French Revolution. But, King Louis XIII had already removed the rood screen, clerics had already whitewashed the walls, and architect Germain Soufflot had already proceeded with some awkward modifications when the *sans-culottes* of the French Revolution destroyed the statues of the kings of Judea decorating the façade because they mistook them for French monarchs.

But the times changed again. Beginning in 1857, Viollet-le-Duc rehabilitated the cathedral. His restoration work was helped by the popularity of Victor Hugo's novel. The public dearly wanted to save the nearly abandoned but legendary church.

With Hugo's *The Hunchback of Notre Dame*, published in 1831, the cathedral forever became the home of Quasimodo the bell ringer, Father Frollo, and the ever lovely Esmeralda.

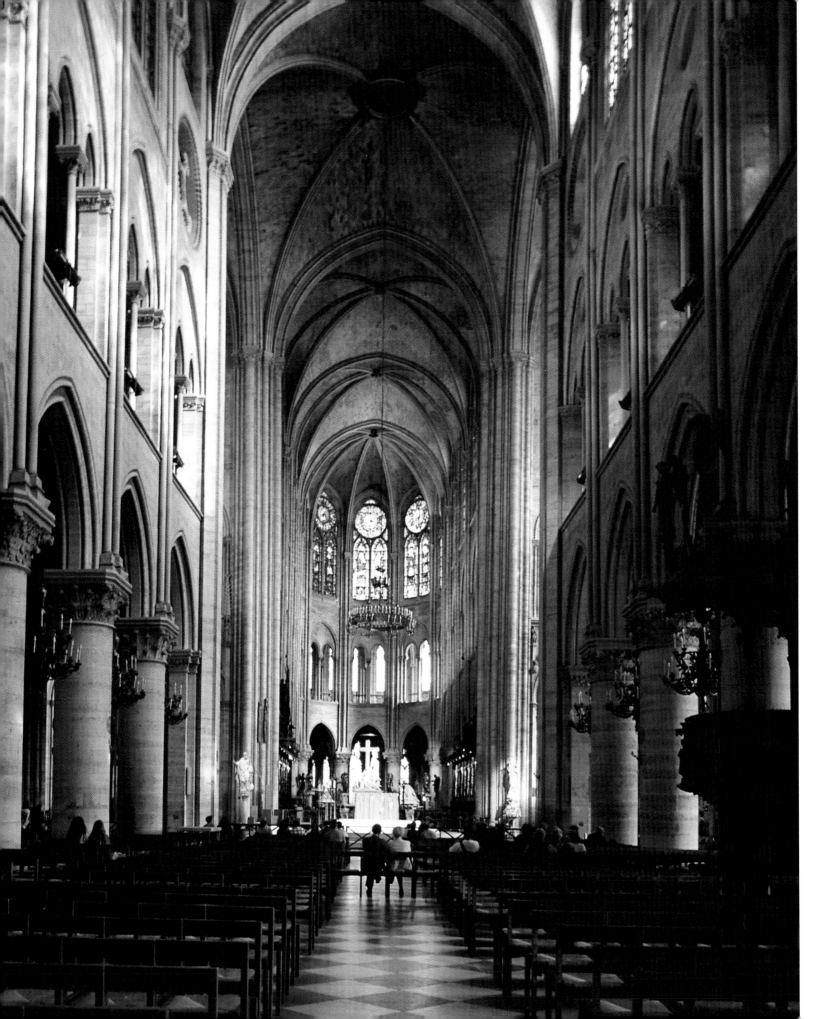

Notre Dame seen from Quai
de la Tournelle.

Opposite: The nave and choir
of Notre Dame.

Square Jean-XXIII, east side
of the cathedral, dedicated
to Pope John XXIII.

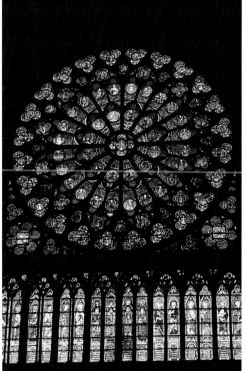

Saint-Étienne portal.

The south rose window
of the transept.

The present-day steeple, rebuilt in 1857, rises nearly 250 feet (75 meters).

Statue of the Virgin Mary, entrance to the chapel.

Opposite: In the upper chapel, the statues of Christ's apostles, veritable pillars of the Church.

La sainte-chapelle and La conciergerie

The Sainte-Chapelle is truly a magnificent example of Gothic art. It practically springs out of its hiding place within the enclosure of the Palais de Justice (the national palace of justice). The chapel was commissioned by Saint Louis for his treasured relics acquired during his crusades to the Holy Land: a splinter of the cross and a fragment of Christ's thorn of crowns. This immense reliquary was built in the mid-13th century. Today, the Sainte-Chapelle is the oldest vestige of the medieval palace built by the kings of France on Île de la Cité. The splendid, slender, flamboyant gothic chapel was constructed on two levels so that the monarch and the royal family would not have to mingle with non-royalty consigned to the ground floor. The stained-glass windows are internationally renowned. The fifteen multicolored windows, covering a total surface of 1,000 square meters (nearly 10,800 square feet), represent over 1,000 scenes from the Old and the New Testaments. Nearby, is the Conciergerie located on the ground floor of the north wing of the Palais de Justice. Four towers overlook the River Seine. The first tower sits on the corner of the Boulevard du Palais. This imposing square tower is the oldest of the four. It dates back to the middle of the 14th century. On its façade facing the boulevard is the oldest clock in Paris, commissioned by King Charles V. The Conciergerie was the largest prison during the French Revolution. Famed names were locked up here to await execution. Today's visitors can peek into Queen Marie-Antoinette's prison cell.

The oldest clock in Paris,
on the Tour Carrée.

Palais de Justice, main gates.

The Conciergerie, north wing, on the banks of the Seine.

White stone and red brick houses framing the triangular park and square.

La Place Dauphine

The delightfully charming Place Dauphine was created to enlarge Île de la Cité by filling in and connecting three sandy islets (l'Île aux Juifs, l'Île des Passeurs de Vaches and l'Îlot de la Gourdaine). On this western tip of the island one of the most gruesome events in Paris history occurred. In 1314 Jacques de Molay, Grand Master of the Knights Templar, was burned alive upon the order of King Philip IV, known as "the Fair" (not at all ironically, for it was "fair" as in handsome). Construction of the Pont Neuf, which crosses over this nose of the island, began in 1578 but was not completed until 1607. King Henri IV then decided to embellish the tiny triangular neighborhood and gave it its present name to honor his son, the future Louis XIII, at that time *Dauphin de France* (heir to the throne). King Henri IV placed the task in the hands of Achille de Harlay, president of the parliament of Paris. Harlay commissioned a closed residential triangle

of 32 identical brick and white stone houses. The eastern end was later demolished to allow a view of the façade of the Palais de Justice. At the western point of the triangle, a gate opened toward the River Seine. In the center, a statue of King Henri IV on horseback watched over the creation. Traditionally, all royal places in Paris were endowed with a statue in honor of their royal sponsor.

Though formal, Place Dauphine is far too charming to come off as stuffy or official. It has always attracted artists and writers like Thomas Mann, Gérard de Nerval, or Georges Simenon whose famous police superintendent Commissaire Maigret frequented the Brasserie Dauphine. Had the fictional Maigret been a real-life person, he might have run into singer Yves Montand or actress Simone Signoret who resided at Place Dauphine in the 1950s.

Statue of King Henri IV on horseback.

LE PONT-NEUF

"As sturdy as the Pont Neuf!" This popular expression is as accurate as ever. Despite its misleading name (literally "new bridge"), the Pont Neuf is the oldest and sturdiest of Paris bridges. It was built for King Henri III to facilitate his commutes between the Louvre Palace and the Saint-Germain-des-Prés abbey. But construction was delayed. Consequently, King Henri IV inaugurated the bridge in 1607, more than 25 years after work had begun.

The Pont Neuf was original in that it was the first Paris bridge with no houses or shops built upon it. In 1688, the *Samaritaine* pump went into action at the base of the second arch of the bridge. It pumped river water to nearby fountains. As its name suggests, it is an homage to the Good Samaritan woman who gave Jesus a drink from Jacob's well.

The Pont Neuf was always very lively. Jugglers, gazette vendors, merchants of all sorts plied their trade on the sidewalks. Actors performed comedies on mini-stages. It was often jokingly said, "No one crosses the bridge without running into a white horse, a monk, and a streetwalker." In the last years of the 20th century, the Pont Neuf was reinvested with madness of the creative sort. The sculptor Christo wrapped the bridge up in thousands of feet of white fabric.

Saint-Louis-en-l'Île church, belfry.

L'île Saint-Louis

This tiny island-village is composed of three east-west streets, and seven north-south streets. An 18th-century church's bell tower watches over the central main street, rue Saint-Louis-en-l'Île. This village is one of the most extraordinary architectural ensembles to be seen in Paris. Ile Saint-Louis was originally two islets, l'île aux Vaches and l'île Notre-Dame which belonged to the monks of the chapter of Notre-Dame. In 1614, a group of developers, Marie, Poulletier & Le Regrattier, were assigned the urban development plan. They were subsequently replaced by a faster and more efficient team of developers, Jean Chevrier and Jean de La Grange. They called upon Louis Le Vau, one of the most prestigious architects of his time, to construct most of the mansions on the quays: the Hôtel Lambert with interior decoration by painter Charles Le Brun, the Hôtel de Lauzun where writer Théophile Gautier founded the Club des Haschischins (the hashish smokers' club which drew the likes of Baudelaire, Barbey d'Aurevilly, Delacroix, Daumier, and Balzac, gathered around a good opium pipe), and the Hôtel Hesselin on Quai de Béthune. Parisian aristocracy quickly moved in to enjoy the pleasures of the island, and snapped up the prestigious mansions. Numerous celebrities have made their homes here: actress Michèle Morgan, French President Georges Pompidou, singer Georges Moustaki, and so many others.

Today, the island is a favorite for Sunday walks. People line up at Berthillon's for the yummiest ice cream in Paris, then, ice cream in hand, stroll over to the artists' studios, art galleries, and artisans' boutiques up and down Rue Saint-Louis-en-l'Île.

Hôtel Lambert, 2, rue Saint-Louis-en-l'Île.

Pont Marie.

La TOUR D'aRGenT

The Hostellerie de la Tour d'Argent, founded in 1582, had the honor of serving King Henri IV a steaming *poule au pot* (a chicken dish) and Madame de Sévigné was served a very refined and rare drink in her time, hot chocolate. Although the original restaurant was destroyed during the Revolution, one of Napoleon III's cooks rebuilt it and turned it into a monument of French gastronomy.

The incomparable view of the River Seine has delighted many newly wed couples including Princess Elizabeth and Philip Duke of Edinburgh. The list of celebrities is long. Queen Ingrid of Denmark, Grace of Monaco, Charlie Chaplin, Woody Allen, Maria Callas, and many more have been seated at the tables of this restaurant with a sweeping vista of Paris.

One of the most highly appreciated specialties is duck. If you have the budget, try the roasted fillets of smothered duckling served with minced liver in Madeira wine, cognac and lemon juice, or the duckling with rennet apples, or duck with pears, or the Montmorency duckling filet. Since 1890, this most prestigious of Paris restaurants has concocted a thousand and one duck recipes. Its wine cellar is so vast the wine list is a thick book.

GOURMET DELIGHTS

Le Train Bleu.

Lucas Carton.

Ledoyen.

L'Escargot Montorgueil.

BRASSERIE LIPP
CHOUCROUTE
JAMBON D'YORK
SAUCISSES DE STRASBOURG
HARENGS MARINÉS
PLAT DU JOUR
VINS
ET
PRODUITS D'ALSACE

Prunier-Traktir.

The first real restaurant in modern terms appeared in Paris in 1791. Méot, a former head cook for the Duke of Orléans, opened a magnificent establishment near the Palais-Royal. Méot offered his guests a menu of one hundred dishes, and a wine list with twenty-two red wines and twenty-seven white wines. Certainly, Paris had its cafés, inns, and taverns, but the fare was invariable. Guests had to elbow and jostle with each other for a sliver of meat off the main course plopped in the middle of the table.

Parisians rushed to "restore" their stomachs and souls at the newfangled "restaurants" that opened at the Palais-Royal like the Café de Chartres (now Le Grand Véfour). Next came the wave of more popular restaurants in the capital. 19th-century Parisians of all walks of life began enjoying the pleasures of regional cuisine. Menus suddenly featured *bouillabaisse* (a Mediterranean specialty) and *brandade de morue* (a codfish dish). On Rue Montorgueil, Le Rocher de Cancale, a favorite among characters in Balzac's novels, is still serving food today. A good number of the prestigious restaurants established at the turn of the 20th century are still going strong: La Pérouse, Prunier, Lucas Carton, and so many more.

Food lovers visiting Paris, whatever your budget or inspiration, you will have plenty of choice: the splendid décor of Le Train Bleu at the *Gare de Lyon* (Lyon train station), the inimitable and popular ambiance of the Bouillon Chartier off the Grands Boulevards, the intact and quaint old-fashioned charm of L'Escargot Montorgueil, the special air at Drouant, site of the annual Prix Goncourt, Maxim's and Fouquet's whose décors have not changed, the large chain of Les Brasseries Bofinger, and the little Polidor restaurant with its checkered tablecloths so reassuringly quaint.

Les Chevaux du Soleil, bas-relief decorating the stables of the Hôtel de Rohan, 87, rue Vieille-du-Temple.

Hôtel Carnavalet, 23, rue de Sévigné.

Le marais

This superb quarter of Paris, studded with numerous 17th- and 18th-century mansions, narrowly escaped demolition in the 1950s. Little by little, workshops and lean-tos had taken over courtyards and alleyways. A miracle occurred in August 1962 when legislators passed the Malraux bill protecting historic sections of the city. The Marais was saved, and gradually rehabilitated. One by one, its mansions shed their gray shadows of neglect.

The Hôtel d'Hallwyll and the Hôtel de Montmor have retained their discretion. But the Hôtel d'Avaux de Saint-Aignan is now open to the public as home to the musée d'Art et d'Histoire du judaïsme (the museum of jewish art and history). Almost in the center of the quarter is the Palais de Soubise, home to the Archives nationales (the national archives). Its northern neighbor, the Hôtel de Clisson, still has its turrets, reminders of its medieval origins. At the intersection of Rue des Archives and Rue des Quatre-Fils stands the Hôtel Guénégaud des Brosses, the work of architect François Mansart. It is now the musée de la Chasse et de la Nature (the museum of hunting and nature). Rue Vieille-du-Temple is also lined with elegant old homes. At number 47, the Hôtel des Ambassadeurs de Hollande has one of the finest carriage entrances in all the Marais. The nearby Hôtel d'Hérouet, at number 54, was not as lucky; a bomb destroyed much of it in August 1944. Further up the street at number 87 is the austere Hôtel de Rohan, enclosed within the Archives nationales (the national archives building).

A side step onto Rue des Francs-Bourgeois brings us to the Hôtel d'Almeras and the Hôtel de Sandreville. Along with the Hôtel d'Albret, Hôtel Lamoignon, Hôtel Donon, they and scores of other splendid mansions belong to the golden age of the Marais. The jewel of Rue des Francs-Bourgeois is the magnificent Hôtel Carnavalet, at the corner of Rue de Sévigné. It was the prestigious home of the Marquise de Sévigné. Today, it houses the musée Carnavalet, museum devoted to the history of the city of Paris.

Picasso lovers will relish a visit to the musée Picasso within the walls of the Hôtel Salé. This 17th-century home was constructed for nouveau riche Pierre Aubert de Fontenay who had made a fortune collecting the tax on salt, hence the mansion's name (literally "salty"). The quarter south of Rue Saint-Antoine equally deserves a leisurely detour. At 68, rue François-Miron is the splendid Hôtel de Beauvais, home of Catherine Bellier, nicknamed "Catheau la Borgnesse" ("One-eyed Cathy"), the lady-in-waiting who made a man of 16-year-old

King Louis XIV. On Rue de Jouy, the Hôtel d'Aumont now houses the administrative tribunal of Paris, while at 62, Rue Saint-Antoine, the palatial Hôtel de Sully is headquarters to the Centre des monuments nationaux (the national office for historical monuments). Pass through its lovely French garden then its Orangerie to enter the arcades of Place des Vosges. Closer to the Seine is the Hôtel de Sens, once a residence of Queen Margot. This rare vestige of the Middle Ages in Paris was restored rather heavy-handedly.

Hôtel Lamoignon,
24, rue Pavée,
headquarters of
the Paris city history
library.

Square George Cain.

Hôtel Lamoignon.

Hôtel de Soubise, 60, rue des Francs-Bourgeois,
Archives nationales.

160, rue Saint-Martin (detail).

Orangerie, Hôtel de Sully,
62, rue Saint-Antoine.

The Picasso Museum, located within the Hôtel Aubert de Fontenay
(a.k.a. Hôtel Salé), 5, rue de Thorigny.

From top to bottom:
Hôtel Donon, 8, rue Elzévir;
Saint-Paul & Saint-Louis church, 99, rue Saint-Antoine;
Hôtel d'Alméras, 30, rue des Francs-Bourgeois.

Hôtel de Bonneval, 16, parc Royal.

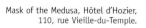

Mask of the Medusa, Hôtel d'Hozier,
110, rue Vieille-du-Temple.

Hôtel de Sens, 1, rue du Figuier.

la place des vosges

The history of the Place des Vosges begins with a tragic accident. During a tournament in front of the Palais des Tournelles, King Henri II was mortally wounded by his opponent's lance. His widow, Queen Catherine de' Medici decided to be rid of the structure that held such bad memories. The vacated space remained unoccupied until King Henri IV ordered a silk factory and a public square on the site. By the grace of the architects (who unfortunately remain anonymous), the square was built with the elegance and harmony that we know today. It was inaugurated with continuous festivities from April 5 to April 7, 1612.

Under the reign of Louis XIII, it took the name Place Royale. A statue of the King on horseback, executed by Cortot and Dupaty, was placed in the center of the square. The name was changed in 1800 to Place des Vosges in honor of the first french *département* to pay taxes due.

Numerous celebrities of Paris social life have taken residence within this harmonious décor. Madame de Sévigné was born in the mansion that belonged to her family at the address 1 bis, Place des Vosges. The actress Rachel, the legendary courtesan Marion Delorme, writers Jacques Bossuet and Alphonse Daudet have lived here. But the greatest literary figure to have lived at Place des Vosges was Victor Hugo. His apartment at number 6 has now been transformed into a museum in his honor.

Equestrian statue of Louis XIII.

Square Louis XIII.

The Grande Colonnade, rue de l'Amiral-de-Coligny.

Le palais du Louvre

Around the year 1200, King Philippe Auguste built a small fortress to reinforce the ramparts he had put up round the capital. Throughout the second millennium, every ruler after him enlarged, embellished, transformed, and often destroyed whole sections, only to improve this palace. After symbolizing absolute divine right of the monarchy, today the Louvre Museum houses masterpieces of art from all periods and all civilizations. The number of transformations is mind-boggling.

Art collector King Charles V was the first to bring in several works of art as well as wild animals. François I, then Henri II transformed the medieval fortress into a palace in line with the tastes of their times. Architect Pierre Lescot composed the first elements of the Renaissance palace. Catherine de' Medici endowed it with a garden attached to her new Tuileries Palace. Construction ground to a halt during the Wars of Religion. Atrocities were committed in the Louvre royal

palace on the night of St. Bartholomew's Day (August 24, 1572). Renovation resumed in 1594 under Henri IV. He continued embellishing the château in which he died in 1610, stabbed in his carriage by François Ravaillac. Until the end of the Fronde (a civil war which began in 1648 as a squabble over restrictions on royal powers), King Louis XIV steered clear of the Louvre. When he returned to Paris, he commissioned architect Le Vau to continue work and Claude Perrault to design the

colonnade. But in 1678, Louis XIV began moving his court to Versailles. His plans for the Louvre were never fully carried out. The former royal residence remained unfinished for a long time.

Napoleon III was the last sovereign to attempt completing the three-centuries-old grand plan of connecting the Louvre to the Tuileries Palace. The work was short-lived. The Communards burned the Tuileries and a wing of the Louvre.

The Louvre was no longer a government palace. It was gradually conquered by the expanding museum. The Finance Ministry was the last representative of state power to be forced out to make room for the world's largest museum.

American architect Ieoh Ming Pei's major transformations and embellishments brought the Louvre its new stature as a world-class museum but also made it one of the most pleasant to walk through. The primary

focus of the project was to create beneath the central courtyard a vast underground reception area, full of light and with corridors facilitating access to the three pavilions of the museum. What the museum needed was a stunning main entrance worthy of this temple of arts. Pei took inspiration from the ancients' vocabulary. Today, his glass and metal pyramid is almost as famous as the works within the Grand Louvre.

The glass pyramid entrance
in the center of the Cour Napoléon.

The Arc du Carrousel celebrates
the military victories of Napoleon I.

The foundations of the medieval Louvre,
on display beneath the present-day palace.

Le musée du Louvre

Mona Lisa, an enigmatic Italian belle, has more admirers than any other young woman in Paris. Every day thousands come to pay their respects, take photographs, and try to cajole a wider smile out of *La Joconde.* But she remains very dignified behind her bulletproof glass. She seems to know her fickle flatterers will slowly back away and move on to gaze upon her rivals, the *Venus de Milo*, or the *Victory of Samothrace.* These are not the only exceptional figures that museum visitors encounter: the contemplative

Egyptian *Scribe*, the majestic *François I*, the large audience attending the *Coronation of Napoleon*, the doomed sailors slipping to a watery death off the sinking *Raft of the Medusa*, or the merry guests at the *Wedding Feats at Cana.*

The Medici Gallery alone offers twenty-four paintings by Rubens recounting the life of Marie de' Medici. The Cour Marly, protected by a glass roof, holds the French statue collection. French and Italian paintings will be found exhibited throughout the Grande Galerie

along the banks of the Seine. Every room, hall, and corridor of the Louvre Museum is chockfull of historic masterpieces.

The idea of devoting part of the Louvre Palace to a museum dates back to the reign of Louis XV. With each succeeding conquest, the museum expanded. Baron Dominique Vivant Denon was the first appointed to organize it. Denon accompanied Bonaparte on the Egyptian campaign, which explains in part the incredibly rich Ancient Egyptian collection at the Louvre.

Jan Vermeer (1632-1675), *The Lacemaker* (c. 1660)
(Ph. RMN/R. G. Ojeda).

Leonardo da Vinci (1452-1519), *Portrait of Lisa Gherandini, known as Mona Lisa* (1503/06) (Ph. RMN/R. G. Ojeda).

Aphrodite, known as the *Venus de Milo*
(c. 100 B.C.) (Ph. RMN/D. Arnaudet ; J. Scho).

From left to right, and from top to bottom:
François Joseph Bosio (1768-1845), *Hercules Slaying Acheloüs, Metamorphosed as a Serpent*, 1823
Antonio Canova (1757-1822), *Eros and Psyche*, 1793
Pierre Puget (1620-1694), *Perseus and Andromeda*, 1678-84
The Bulls of Khorsabad, Assyrian, circa 720 B.C.

Opposite:
The Victory of Samothrace, circa 190 B.C.

Aristide Maillol (1861-1944), *La Rivière*.

Les Tuileries

Voluptuous ladies hide in the greenery of this garden. Forever frozen in time, *La Baigneuse à la draperie* and *Les trois nymphes* stand near *Venus*, *La Baigneuse se coiffant*, and *La Jeune fille allongée*. Since 1964, the Carrousel garden has been the home for an ensemble of statues by Aristide Maillol, originally from the foundation set up by his former model and inspiration, Dina Vierny. Between the two wings of the Louvre, lovely bronze feminine figures seem to guard the entrance to the Tuileries.

The clay soil of the gardens served in the manufacture of roof tiles ("tuiles"), hence the name, Les Tuileries. In 1664, landscape artist Le Nôtre designed the grand garden that stretches from the Louvre to Place de la Concorde. His original plan has been fairly accurately restored. On both sides of the broad central garden path, groves of linden and chestnut trees shade small kiosks where you can get a cup of expresso from spring to autumn. The northern pathway called La Terrasse des Feuillants is a testimony to the French Revolution. In 1791, one of the moderate groups (or "clubs" to use the precise term) in the National Assembly was called Les Feuillants because it usually met in a hall in the former Feuillants convent just off Rue de Rivoli. Two museums frame the western garden gates onto Place de la Concorde. La Galerie nationale du Jeu de Paume exhibits contemporary art; it was formerly the site of a court for the granddaddy of the squash game. It was built for Napoleon III. Opposite it, Monet's *Les Nymphéas* occupy two rooms of the Musée de l'Orangerie. Toy boats with colorful sails glide across the octagonal fountain called *Le Grand Bassin*, only a stone's throw from Place de la Concorde.

The garden on the Rue de Rivoli side.
In the background: the north wing of the Louvre
and its Pavillon de Marsan, place des Pyramides.

The octagonal fountain at the garden entrance
from place de la Concorde.

Pont des Arts.

Passerelle Debilly, footbridge.

Piers of the Pont des Arts.

Pont Marie.

PARIS BRIDGES

The Pont Neuf is the oldest while the Passerelle Solférino (footbridge) connecting the Musée d'Orsay and the Tuileries is the most recent. The bridges of Paris, their construction, their destruction sometimes, are integral parts of the history of this city founded by sailors on the banks and islands of the River Seine. Still today, the rhythm of day-to-day life in the capital is set by the mood of the river.

For centuries, Parisians had to ferry across the river.

But by the end of the Middle Ages, several bridges had gone up, all fragile wooden structures encumbered with houses and shops. Fires were frequent. Some bridges were swept downstream by huge blocks of ice during harsh winters. Others suffered serious damage from collisions by drifting boats.

Each century has given Paris at least a few feats of engineering spanning the Seine. Many are milestones in Paris history. The Concorde bridge recalls the

disturbances of the French Revolution. Stones from the demolished Bastille were incorporated in upper portions of its piers. The Pont de Bir-Hakeim was built for the Universal Exhibition of 1878. In the center of Paris, the first stone for the construction of the Pont Alexandre-III was laid by Czar Nicholas II. As for the Pont de l'Alma, since the great flood of 1910, its statue of a Zouave on one of the piers has been a favorite of Parisians checking the level of the Seine.

Passerelle Solférino
and Pont Alexandre-III.

Pont au Double, Petit-Pont, and Pont Saint-Michel.

Pont Charles-de-Gaulle, viaduct, and Pont d'Austerlitz.

ORSAY, THE TRAIN STATION TURNED MUSEUM

Other than the façade's statues representing the cities of Toulouse, Bordeaux, and Nantes, it was a long time before any pieces of art pulled into the Orsay train station. This monument to the glory of the great 19th-century invention of railed transportation opened on July 14, 1900. It was built on the ruins of the Orsay Palace, the Foreign Affairs Ministry, which was burned down by revolutionaries in 1871, during the Commune de Paris. After it stopped serving as a train station in 1939, its future long remained uncertain. There were plans to raze it or even to turn it into a hotel. It was used as an auction house, and a theater for Madeleine Renault and Jean-Louis Barrault's troop. Orson Wells shot his 1963 film *The Trial* here. Then at the end of the 1970s, everything changed. The former Orléans railway company's station became one of the largest and best-endowed museums in Paris – a celebration of 19th-century art. Orsay Museum was inaugurated in December 1986 and now welcomes some highly illustrious passengers.

Some of France's most prestigious works of art have been displayed in the halls redesigned by Gae Aulenti. Visitors are captivated first by the seductive diaphanous curves of *La Naissance de Vénus (Birth of Venus)*, by Alexandre Cabanel, one of the many paintings representing the official art and the official taste of the Second Empire. Works by Gustave Moreau, Puvis de Chavannes, and Paul Baudry rival more austere pieces such as Gustave Courbet's famous *L'Enterrement à Ornans (Burial at Ornans)*. Other rooms are devoted to the impressionists, featuring pieces by Monet, Picasso, and Berthe Morisot. Manet's *Olympia* was severely criticized upon its first public display. Gustave Caillebotte's *Les Raboteurs de parquet (The Floor-Scrapers)* was deemed trivial. *Le bal du Moulin de la Galette* by Pierre-Auguste Renoir draws us into a whirlwind. Van Gogh meets Cézanne.

Works by the Pont-Aven school of painters (with Gauguin at its head) neighbor works by Toulouse-Lautrec, Seurat, and Signac.

We have come a long way since smoking locomotives chugged their way toward southwestern France.

Gustave Moreau (1826-1898),
Galatée, 1880 (Ph. RMN/R. G. Ojeda).

Gustave Courbet (1819-1877),
Un enterrement à Ornans (1849/50)
(Ph. RMN/H. Lewandowski).

Claude Monet (1840-1926),
Coquelicots, environs d'Argenteuil, 1873
(Ph. RMN/H. Lewandowski).

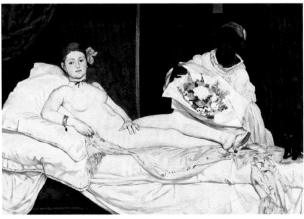

Édouard Manet (1832-1863),
Olympia, 1863
(Ph. RMN/H. Lewandowski).

Vincent Van Gogh (1853-1890),
Autoportrait, 1889
(Ph. RMN/G. Blot).

Paul Cézanne (1839-1906), *Pommes et oranges*
(1895/1900) (Ph. RMN/H. Lewandowski).

Paul Gauguin (1848-1903),
Femmes de Tahiti ou *Sur la plage,* 1891
(Ph. RMN/H. Lewandowski).

Gustave Caillebotte (1848-1894),
Les Raboteurs de parquet (1875)
(Ph. RMN/H. Lewandowski).

Édouard Manet (1832-1883),
*Berthe Morisot au bouquet
de violettes* (1872).

Henri de Toulouse-Lautrec
(1864-1901), *La Clownesse
Cha-U-KO, artiste au Moulin
Rouge,* 1895.

Auguste Renoir (1841-1919),
*Bal du Moulin de la Galette,
Montmartre* (1876)
(Photos RMN/H. Lewandowski).

Le centre
Georges-Pompidou

The Forum.

The Stravinski fountain.

The Piazza.

Aptly named "Beau Bourg", this was one of many pretty outlying boroughs incorporated into Paris when King Philippe Auguste enclosed the medieval city with ramparts in 1213. The old Saint-Merri church and a few period houses still standing today recall the bustle of bygone days.

In the 19th century, city officials laid out broad new streets and boulevards that seriously bit into the medieval enclave. Locked behind the likes of the new and thriving Boulevard Sébastopol and Rue Rambuteau, the old quarter fell into neglect. It was so run down by the early 1970s, a clean sweep was made. President Georges Pompidou was an amateur of modern art. Thus, a contemporary arts museum went up on the cleared site: "The Pompidou Center" is short form for the Musée national d'art moderne (the national museum of modern art). Critics sneered. Citizens jeered. It certainly deserved its moniker, "the oil refinery." Architects Renzo Piano and Richard Rogers took a radical approach: Push all the conduits, air shafts, and bearing structures out to the façade, the glass-covered tunnel-escalator included! But every day, thousands of people rush to visit the museum. The success has been phenomenal, and rightly so. Over the years, the museum has offered exciting, high-quality, permanent and temporary exhibitions featuring major works of contemporary art. This architectural oddity in the heart of a revived Paris district has become one of the most famous and visited monuments of the city.

Le musée national d'art moderne

MNAM, or the National Museum of Modern Art, offers numerous collections of contemporary art. The museum's vast holdings represent all the great artistic movements of the 20th century, from Cubism to Pop Art.

Ugo Rondinone (1964-), *The evening passes like any other men and women float alone through the air...*, 1999 (©Adagp, Paris 2002, photo G. Meguerditchian).

Yves Klein (1928-1962), *Grande anthropophagie bleue, Hommage à Tennessee Williams*, 1960 (Coll. Centre Pompidou, Musée national d'art moderne, ©Adagp, Paris 2002, photo Cnac/Mnam, dist. RMN).

Vassily Kandinsky (1866-1944), *Gelb-Rot-Blau*, 1925 (©Adagp, Paris 2002, photo Ph. Migeat).

Giuseppe Penone (1947-), *Respirer l'ombre*, 2000 (Coll. Cnac/Mnam, dist. RMN, ©Adagp, Paris 2002, photo Ph. Migeat).

Xavier Veilhan (1963-), *Le Rhinocéros, 1999*
(© Adagp, Paris 2002, © Cnac/Mnam,
photo G. Meguerditchian).

Joan Miró (1893-1983), *Tête d'homme, 1935,*
(©Cnac/Mnam, dist. RMN, photo J.-C. Planchet,
©Adagp, Paris 2002).

Henri Matisse (1869-1954), *Grand Intérieur rouge,*
1948, (© Succession Matisse, 2002, photo Cnac/Mnam).

Frank Stella (1936-), *Mas o Manos,* 1964
et *Polombe,* 1994 (©Cnac/Mnam, photo P. Migeat).

THE RIVER Seine

Paris, city of ports. Every day, barges transport
thousands of tons of merchandise through the capital.
The inhabitants of ancient Lutetia were *nautes*,
a guild of cargo riverboat sailors.
Paris, city of water. The river is connected to every
major event in Paris history. In the darkest hours of
that history, it was upon the Seine that the Norman
invaders threateningly and skillfully maneuvered

their *drakkars*. In 1910, the raging floodwaters of the Seine caused the most dramatic damage of the 20th century. For days, the river seemed intent on reclaiming its prehistoric riverbed, wreaking havoc for Parisians who had forgotten that the river once flowed where the Grands Boulevards were laid out.
The Seine long provided drinking water for Paris, despite the poor quality. Boats and barges loaded with produce for the numerous markets set up along the river also brought barrels of wine to be sold at the Bercy warehouses and the Halle aux Vins. Today, the Seine tempts lovers with romantic boat rides or long strolls along its quays. The River Seine will forever be an integral part of Parisian life, by day and by night.

THE EIFFEL TOWER

When Paris decided to host the Universal Exhibition in 1889 as a centennial celebration of the storming of the Bastille, government minister Jules Ferry launched the idea for an extraordinary monument 1,000 feet high. At the time, the challenge seemed quite impossible as the world's highest monument, the Washington Monument, already reached a daring 555'6" inches (169 meters). Seven hundred projects vied for the honor of serving as the exhibition's centerpiece, but Gustave Eiffel's tower was the obvious choice. Eiffel was no anonymous engineer at the time. He had already proven his talents with his spectacular metal bridges for Garabit in central France and for Porto in Portugal. He was also given the honor of designing the framework for the Statue of Liberty in New York. 2.5 million rivets and 15,000 metal sections went into the construction of the tower. The work proceeded at an astounding record-breaking pace. Barely two years after work began, on March 31, 1889, Gustave Eiffel personally hoisted the French flag from the top of the third story. In the first year it was open to the public, nearly 2 million people rushed to visit the monument. One wonders how many of them actually had the courage and stamina to climb all 1,672 steps to the top.

The Eiffel Tower has served multiple purposes: a broadcast antenna, a military observatory during World War I, a billboard for automobile manufacturer Citroën in the 1930s, an aircraft beacon in 1947, and a gigantic chronometer counting down the days and minutes to the year 2000. On December 31, 1999 at 11:59 P.M., the Eiffel Tower lit up the night sky with breathtaking fireworks to welcome in the year 2000. But is not the essential function of the elegant "Iron Lady," still today and forever more, to be the symbol of Paris for the whole world?

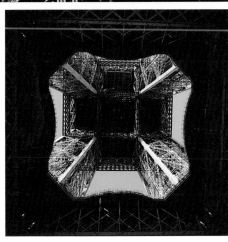

Le Trocadéro

Throughout history, the Chaillot hillock has attracted many architectural fantasies. Architects drew up plans to glorify the French Monarchy, or celebrate the exploits of Napoleon I with a column 30 meters high, or place the Emperor's remains in an immense mausoleum inspired by that of Roman Emperor Augustus.

For the 1878 Universal Exhibition, architects Davioud and Bourdais designed the Trocadéro Palace. This odd Moorish-style monument, composed of a rotunda and two flanking minarets, was supposed to be temporary.

But it stood in place until replaced in 1937 by the Palais de Chaillot, designed by architects Carlu, Boileau, and Azéma for the Universal Exhibition of that year. The new palace was as grandiose, imposing, and monumental as its predecessor had been strange, incongruous, and vaguely ridiculous. The Palais de Chaillot houses museums and cultural organizations: le musée de l'Homme (museum of mankind), le musée de la Marine (naval museum), le musée des Monuments français (soon to be the Cité de l'Architecture), le théâtre

national de Chaillot (the Chaillot national theater), and the Cinémathèque française (museum of cinematography).

The palace's two wings embrace gardens on the sloping river bank, and frame the vast Esplanade des Droits de l'Homme, dedicated to human rights as the name indicates, offering a truly magnificent view of the Eiffel Tower and the Champ-de-Mars across the Seine.

On hot summer days, children splash joyfully in the Trocadéro fountains.

LES INVALIDES

Upper galleries, Cour d'Honneur.

The Esplanade des Invalides.

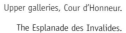

Dôme des Invalides church.

The Jardin de l'Intendant.

Parole portée, sculpture and fountain
by Nicolas Alquin.

King Louis XIV established this institution as a veterans' hospital and hospice. In its first years of operation the establishment had between 5,000 and 7,000 pensioners. Some were assigned to tend the superintendent's vegetable patch. Parisians would frequently come chat with the old soldiers hoeing rows of lettuce. But about 150 years ago, the monument changed vocations and became the final resting place for Emperor Napoleon I. His remains were placed under the dome in a sumptuous tomb made of Russian porphyry.

The emperor's only son (Napoleon II, also known as L'Aiglon, the eaglet) and eldest brother Joseph have their final resting places beneath the gilded dome. Marshal Ferdinand Foch, general of the allied armies during the First World War, was laid to rest here. When architect Jules Hardouin-Mansart designed the chapel beneath the dome, he could not have possibly imaged that it would later become an imperial mausoleum.

Initially a charity organization, Les Invalides has since become a giant monument to the glory of France's most illustrious generals and military exploits. The Cour d'Honneur still serves today for military ceremonies.

The Museum of the Army is housed within the buildings surrounding this courtyard. The museum's unique collections include the armors of King François I, Louis XIII, and Louis XIV, items from World War I and World War II. All around the buildings, numerous cannons captured from defeated enemies recall the glory of the Napoleonic era.

And yet, when sunlight brashly reflects off the gilded dome, when youths transform the wide lawns of the esplanade into soccer fields, the roar of the cannons is forgotten.

Lazing beside the Grand Bassin.

Beehive.

Le Jardin
du Luxembourg

What a fascinating monument the de' Medici fountain is with its graceful fairy-tale décor. The name helps visitors identify the first owner of the Luxembourg Palace and gardens. "Ah, but was it Marie or Catherine de' Medici?" they frequently ask. In 1615, Queen Marie de' Medici commissioned a residence in an architectural style reminiscent of her native Florence, Italy. Willingly or unwillingly, many major historic figures succeeded her as residents. During the French Revolution, prisoners included Danton and future Empress Joséphine de Beauharnais. Later, her husband Napoleon I chose to reside here for a while.
The property next passed into the hands of King

Louis XVIII who opened the grounds to the public, turning a princely estate into an elaborate public garden. While senators now occupy the palace, the most famous residents of the Luxembourg Gardens are statues. Venus, Minerva, Charles Baudelaire, Stendhal, Paul Verlaine, Queen Mary Stuart, Queen Blanche of Castile, along with dozens of others, stand frozen in time on their pedestals gazing at the swarms of busy (or snoozing) park visitors. Apiculture enthusiasts can learn all about beehives; horticulture classes are held in the orchards. Dozens of chess amateurs gather beside the Orangerie. The Luxembourg Gardens' tennis courts are among the most popular in the capital. Nevertheless,

the hands-down favorite activity amid the greenery is reading in the sunshine. On the first sunny days of spring, wooden and wrought-iron chairs are besieged by Parisians in want of serenity. Students, professors, tourists, and folks of all stripes push through the gates, book in hand. In summer, music lovers replace readers. The music kiosk hosts numerous concerts. But the real reason for the popularity of Luxembourg Gardens is undoubtedly because the park inspires the eternal games that lovers play: flirting, courting, and tender conversation in the shade of magnificent old trees.

Homage to students of the Résistance.

Observatory gardens.

The de' Medici fountain.

The Marie de' Medici Palace.

Place de la Sorbonne, the entrance to
Paris' oldest and most famous university.

Opposite:
Fountain, place Saint-Michel.

THE Latin Quarter

The limits of this tiny principality within the heart of Paris are defined by la Rue des Écoles on the north side of the time-honored Sorbonne and the Boulevard Saint-Michel with its bookshop trade of college and school manuals. A few dozen streets on the slopes of the Montagne Sainte-Geneviève make up the Latin Quarter. It earned this name because Latin was long the language of instruction in the prestigious colleges, universities and secondary schools huddled here. From the Middle Ages until May 1968, students and professors in this erudite enclave of the capital had a well-earned reputation for rowdy, raucous living. The emblem of the Latin Quarter is not the Pantheon, nor the impressive City Hall of the 5th *arrondissement*, but the Sorbonne.

The famed temple of knowledge owes its name to its 13th-century founder Robert de Sorbon, King Louis IX's chaplain, a man who provided housing for needy students. The chapel within the Sorbonne was greatly honored to serve as the burial place of the 17th-century university rector, Cardinal de Richelieu. Over the centuries, the modest college grew to become the impressive university that we know today. Most of its buildings were built at the end of the 19th century around the amphitheater decorated by Puvis de Chavannes. The amphitheater hosts important events, receptions, and colloquiums. However, milestones in the Latin Quarter's history have always occurred in the Sorbonne's central courtyard (or "cour d'honneur" as it is called in French). The statues of Victor Hugo and Louis Pasteur have witnessed numerous student uprisings, notably that of May 1968.

Rue Bourbon-le-Château.

Courtyard off Rue du Cherche-Midi.

Opposite:
Saint-Germain-des-Prés church.

SAINT-GERMAIN-DES-PRÉS

After France's Liberation in 1945, the sidewalk cafés Le Flore and Les Deux Magots became the center of the world for over a decade. The Saint-Germain-des-Prés quarter, a quaint square and a few narrow streets under the shadow of a medieval church, attracted young people, intellectuals, tourists, and jazz musicians. Writer-musician-scientist Boris Vian and Juliette Gréco, a night owl prior to becoming a chanteuse, were two of the major postwar figures in the Saint-Germain-des-Prés arena, as were Jean-Paul Sartre and Simone de Beauvoir, writers and existentialist philosophers. Certain neighborhood bars' basements became swinging nightclubs. Le Tabou and Le Lorientais attracted be-bop dancers hopping to the rhythms of Claude Luter's band, while neighboring cabarets gave young aspiring actors their first start in show business.

Ironically, this quarter famed for its night life, music, and youth, was almost entirely constructed on church property. The Saint-Germain-des-Prés abbey was a veritable fortified village, protected by ramparts. The church is among the oldest in the capital. Portions date back to the year 1000, and foundations of a Merovingian basilica were uncovered near the abbey. Today, Saint-Germain-des-Prés has evolved. Change is inevitable. Several of its large cafés and prestigious bookshops have now vanished and been replaced by fashionable ready-to-wear clothing boutiques. But tables are still being set at Chez Lipp (a favorite among politicians), and drinks are still being served at the sidewalk café Les Deux Magots. Although the ambiance has disappeared, Saint-Germain-des-Prés is as beautiful and charming as ever.

Saint-Eustache church.

Rue du Jour.

Rue Coquillière.

Restaurant Au Pied de Cochon.

Les Halles

Les Halles in the heart of Paris, served for centuries as a gigantic wholesale food market. Thousands of tons of food were transported daily to be traded beneath the iron and glass pavilions designed by architect Victor Baltard. The "belly of Paris" is no more. Despite the exile to the distant suburb of Rungis, this quarter perpetuates an ancient tradition. Business is still thriving. Many fashion designers moved into premises on Rue Pierre-Lescot and Rue du Jour. Lively food markets can still be found on Rue Montorgueil. But the real hum of business went underground to the lower levels of the modern Forum des Halles. Architects Claude Vasconi and Georges Pencreach laid out shopping arcades on the levels above the metro and RER transit network. A central garden courtyard 13 meters below street level brings daylight into the arcades. Movie theaters, a swimming pool, and a video library are but a few of the attractions in this underground city within the city. The entire metropolitan area converges beneath the Forum des Halles. The city's largest shopping mall sits atop the nation's busiest public transportation lines.

Sculpture by Pol Bury.

Le Palais-Royal

In 1629, Cardinal de Richelieu built a palace half a block north of the Louvre so he could be near the seat of power he was serving in his own best interests. He appointed architect Jacques Lemercier and the king's gardener, Desgots, who designed what was to be the largest garden in Paris. Richelieu craftily circumvented any jealousy on the part of the king by simply donating the "Palais Cardinal" to Louis XIII. After Richelieu's death, the new palace occupants were Queen Anne of Austria and her young son, the future Louis XIV; thus, the "Palais Cardinal" became the "Palais Royal." The garden is a paradise for amateurs of calm, giving

them the impression of being isolated from the cares of the outside world. And yet, few Paris monuments symbolize so well movement, agitation, revolt, or the fight for freedom of thought and expression. After Louis XIV left Paris for Versailles, Regent Philippe d'Orléans imbued the palace with its reputation for splendor and decadence. He held gargantuan libertine fêtes. But his grandson, Louis Philippe d'Orléans deserves credit for transforming the palace into a place of debauchery. Needing to settle certain debts, he conceived the idea of expanding the palace and leasing portions of the covered galleries to commerce.

Some of the shops became taverns frequented by ladies of the night and the first revolutionaries. After 1789, it was renamed "Palais Égalité" (equality palace). The name did not last long. In 1825, a new Duke of Orléans, the future King Louis-Philippe, had the wooden galleries torn down and replaced with the beautiful colonnades we know today. Calm returned to the palace. Dignified businesses, the Comédie-Française, and the Ministry of Culture moved in beside the palace. There was no agitation to speak of until the controversial columns of Buren rose from the courtyard pavement.

Daniel Buren's columns, in the central courtyard.

Galerie Véro-Dodat.

Passage du Caire.

Passage des Panoramas.

Passage du Commerce.

arcades

Galerie Véro-Dodat, Passage Jouffroy, Passage des Panoramas and so many other covered alleyways and shopping arcades enrich the capital. Shoppers can fold up their umbrellas and their worries for a stroll down charming indoor lanes and discover the hidden charms of another Paris.

Most of these Parisian passageways were built between 1823 and 1828. More were commissioned between 1839 and 1847 by landlords who wanted to enhance properties and profits by attracting more merchants and more customers. Shops line the long covered galleries that wind through the heart of the property lots. Decorative stained-glass roofs gaily filter daylight. One of the very first arcades, the Passage du Caire

(now serving the wholesale clothing trade), was built on the site of the legendary Cour des Miracles, a veritable slum-principality long ruled by thugs. Twenty-some more arcades went up, mainly in the 1st, 2nd, 9th, and 10th *arrondissements*. While some presently seem to be hibernating (in serious need of rehabilitation), others are bustling with activity. Take the case of the Passage Jouffroy. Visitors of the musée Grévin exit the famed wax museum right into this arcade. An impassive guardian may startle some – but not to worry, the wax figure will be stuck reading his newspaper for many years to come! Bookstores, antique toyshops, and the cozy Hôtel Chopin border this unique artery of Paris.

Each arcade has its own personality. The Passage des Panoramas is the busiest; people come to eat and to listen to street singers. The Galerie Vivienne is the most refined; prim despite the stylish Jean-Paul Gaultier boutique. The Galerie Véro-Dodat is home to fine antique shops. The Passage du Grand-Cerf, which opens onto the boisterous Rue Saint-Denis, features the work of young up-and-coming designers. The covered arcades of Paris are as lively as when they first saw the day. Should the ghost of Nadja (poet André Breton's muse) ever return, she would certainly feel right at home.

Passage Brady.

Galerie Vivienne.

Passage Jouffroy.

Passage des Princes.

L'opéRa-GaRnieR

"What is this style? It is neither classical Greek nor Louis XVI." "No," replied architect Charles Garnier to Empress Eugénie, "it is Napoleon III."
This conversation reportedly took place in 1861 when the imperial couple viewed the model for the Opéra de Paris. Whether factual or not, it neatly sums up the impressions of visitors viewing the edifice for the first time. The opera house, inaugurated in 1875, looked like nothing ever seen previously - a bric-a-brac mishmash of varying artistic trends.
And yet it is so merry, so light. The grand staircase in green Swedish marble seems so appropriately designed

for the wispy rustle of crinoline gowns. The grand foyer decorated with paintings by Paul Baudry is a perfect "drawing-room" backdrop for stylish ladies' gay conversations. The scarlet and gold auditorium prepares the audience for the opulence of the performances. Velvet-lined boxes cushion the hushed remarks of their occupants or the discreet whisperings of young lovers. On the rooftop, a gilded statue of Apollo lifting his lyre skywards dominates the ensemble. On the façade is a copy of *La Danse*, a magnificent composition by sculptor Jean-Baptiste Carpeaux. It sparked quite a controversy. Esthetes of the time called it vulgar.

An outraged critic hurled a bottle of ink at one of the dancing figures to protest the "obscenity" of the piece. The opera house is a prime example of Second Empire taste. Perhaps a bit too much for our contemporaries, for in 1964, Culture Minister André Malraux had the original ceiling by Lenepveu replaced by a Marc Chagall work paying homage to the most famous operas and ballets performed here: *The Magic Flute, Pelleas and Melisande, Tristan and Isolde, The Firebird, Swan Lake, Giselle, Boris Godunov, Romeo and Juliette, Daphnis and Chloé.*

High atop the monumental opera house,
Apollo raises his golden lyre to the heavens.

Top right: the grand staircase. Bottom right: the foyer.

La Place De La Concorde

Navy headquarters seen
from the Jardin des Tuileries.

Luxor Obelisk.

North fountain (detail).

The Luxor obelisk is the centerpiece of the world's most elegant square. Originally part of the Temple of Amon-Re in Thebes, it was a gift to France from Egypt's Viceroy Mehemet Ali, and was erected on the square on October 25, 1836 after a very long trip. A gilded pyramidal tip atop the obelisk glows in the light of the sun while sea nymphs and tritons bathe in the glimmering waters of adjacent fountains representing river and maritime transport.

The land was on the city outskirts when King Louis XV commissioned architect Jacques-Ange Gabriel to lay out this quadrilateral space. Gabriel erected two palaces to flank Rue Royale. One of them contained the royal furniture storehouse before becoming the Navy headquarters. The second palace has since become the world famous Hôtel Crillon, a luxurious meeting place

for illustrious guests. In 1919, the League of Nations pact was drafted in the drawing rooms of this stunning hotel. More recently, and more prosaically, it was on a balcony overlooking Place de la Concorde that France's victorious soccer team presented their trophy to wildly cheering crowds of Parisians.

The three remaining sides of the square are bordered by the River Seine, the Tuileries and Champs-Elysées Gardens. A legion of statues greets visitors. Eight sturdy female figures represent France's eight major cities surrounded by other allegorical figures. The statue representing the city of Strasbourg bears the features of Juliette Drouet, who, before becoming Victor Hugo's

companion, had posed as a model for her beloved, the sculptor J.-J. Pradier. Architect Jacques Hittorf placed maritime rostrum columns as a reminder of the city's emblem, the boat that never sinks.

This monumental square has seen its share of horrors. During the Revolution, guillotine victims at Place de la Concorde included King Louis XVI, Queen Marie-Antoinette, and Charlotte de Corday, famous for having stabbed to death Marat in his bathtub. Later, the guillotine fell on the necks of Robespierre and numerous other artisans of the reign of Terreur during the Revolution. Those gruesome events seem so far away nowadays. Heavy automobile traffic has replaced the cries of the madding masses. Unmoved by clamoring crowds and honking horns, the ancient Luxor obelisk peacefully watches over Paris.

Rue Royale, leading
to the Madeleine church.

The Champs-Élysées, the world's most beautiful avenue and the world-famous Arc de triomphe.

The Champs-Élysées.

Top left: *La Marseillaise*, sculpted by Rude.
Bottom left: *The Victory of Napoleon in 1810,* sculpted by Cortot.

L'ARC DE TRIOMPHE

Every evening at 6 o'clock, a delegation of veterans from one of the wars of the 20th century comes to rekindle the flame at the Arc de triomphe. It has been so since November 11, 1920 when this monument to the glory of Napoleon's armies became the tomb of an unknown soldier from the First World War.

The decision to construct the arch was taken by Emperor Napoleon I in 1806. However, the monument was not completed and inaugurated until 1836 by King Louis-Philippe. In the space of those thirty years, France had seen the fall of the Empire, two kings, and one revolution.

Since then, the Arc de triomphe has been associated with all the major events in the history of the country. When the ashes of Napoleon were brought back from St. Helena Island on December 15, 1840, the procession was marched through the Arc de triomphe, as was Victor Hugo's coffin during his sumptuous funeral, held on May 22, 1885. When World War I ended, in November 1919, the victory parade marched through the Arc de triomphe. To protest the lack of homage paid to WW1 ace fighter pilots, aviator Charles Godefroy daringly flew his plane through the Arc de triomphe. During World War II, the Arc de triomphe was successively a symbol of defeat when Nazi troops marched through it in June 1940, a symbol of the Résistance when demonstrating students marched through on November 11, 1940, and a symbol of final victory on August 26, 1944 when General de Gaulle bowed at the Arc de Triomphe after the battles for the Liberation of Paris.

All these events took place under the stony watch of the figures in the monumental sculpture by François Rude, *Le Départ des Volontaires de 1792*. This piece is also known as *La Marseillaise*, a name that evokes the eternal destiny of the Arc de triomphe in its service to the French Republic.

The Champs-Elysées, the world's most beautiful avenue, still hums with the hustle and bustle of Parisians and visitors to the city. Large department stores, mansions now turned into banks and airline companies' offices, sidewalk cafés, chic Avenue Montaigne with its haute-couture fashion houses, cool refreshing gardens, the imperturbable statue of Clemenceau on the Rond-Point des Champs-Elysées, the metal structures of the Grand Palais and Petit Palais (souvenirs of the 1900 Universal Exhibition), all the décor is there for a fabulous stroll in the City of Lights.

la Défense

The Grande Arche, the monumental steps, suspended canvas, and panoramic-view elevators.

The Arche de la Défense is a "window on the world." Since its 1989 inauguration for the bicentennial of the French Revolution, it has drawn thousands of visitors annually to the exciting La Défense business district. There is no other building like it in the world. It is a nearly perfect cube, 110 meters (352 feet) per side. Its Danish designer, architect Johan Otto Von Spreckelsen, died too young to see his work finished. Inside this hollow cube, architect Paul Andreu designed a suspended Teflon canvas composition that acts as a much-needed windbreak. Four transparent elevators take visitors up to the top for a dizzying panorama. The Arche de la Défense is the third arch of triumph on a slightly curved but historic axis through Paris. The Arche sits at an angle, somewhat askew of the axis, which begins at the Louvre. But its main difference with the Arc du Carrousel and the Arc de triomphe on Place de l'Étoile is that the Arche de la Défense has occupants. On weekdays, over 2,000 government workers from the Ministry of Public Works stream into their offices while exhibitions are being held on the rooftop of the building and students are learning the intricacies of European institutions in the basement library.

But the liveliest part of the building is at its base. With the first pretty days of spring, hundreds of people flock to the steps of the esplanade for lunch-hour picnics, turning the Arche de la Défense into the largest park bench in the metropolitan region.

Charles-de-Gaulle Esplanade, the heart of the business district.

Passerelle de l'Iris, footbridge.

The CNIT building's concrete vaults.

The giant *Thumb*, by sculptor César.

Metro station Porte Dauphine
in the 16th arrondissement.

Castel Béranger (details),
14, rue La Fontaine.

Gate, Hôtel Mezzara, 60, rue La Fontaine.

One of the most intriguing buildings in Paris stands at 14, rue La Fontaine in the 16th *arrondissement*. Le Castel Béranger has an intricate façade: foliage and flowers, vines and branches seem to jut out from the stone. The Castel was built between 1894 and 1898 as a low-income housing investment. Architect Hector Guimard made it a veritable work of art without exceeding the budget allotted him for the project. Guimard designed every element of the building: fantastic arabesques for the doors, windows, doorknobs, and wallpaper. Guimard was the father of what would be called Modern French style. His creations were hardly greeted with unanimous public acclaim. Consequently, his next buildings were much tamer in spirit, as witnessed by two hotels he designed on Avenue Mozart and Rue La Fontaine. However, Guimard had great success in the decorative arts. He made quite a name for himself in furniture design. Guimard is generally considered one of the precursors of Art Deco. Despite the vicissitudes of his career, he made a lasting mark on the urban landscape of the capital. Hector Guimard was selected to design the metro entrances for the first lines that opened in 1899. Several remain in place today. The Porte Dauphine metro station is the best-preserved example. The stairs are encased in a sort of glass butterfly made of panels of enameled lava rock set in a cast-iron structure.

The Guimard metro stations, like the Wallace fountains and the Hittorf street lamps, have now become part of the architectural heritage of Paris, on equal footing with the most prestigious monuments.

The Thinker in the gardens of the Musée Rodin.

Campanile and pool at Parc Georges-Brassens.

The Parc Floral de Paris.

Arboretum in the Bois de Vincennes.

Paris Gardens

How far away the city seems when seen from the broad alleys of the Jardin des Plantes. How pleasant it is to do nothing but soak up the sun on the lawns at the Parc André-Citroën. Children seem so happy in the tiniest sandbox. Paris is a garden. The city has 400 green spaces. Priority was given to setting up public gardens by almost every monarch and head of state. The Tuileries,

Luxembourg, Palais-Royal, are all part of official grand designs to please the population. Napoleon III rightly deserves to be called the "Garden Emperor." After a first exile in London, he returned to France with a penchant for the vast landscaped parks of England. He launched the fashion in Paris. The Emperor commissioned the Parc Montsouris, the Buttes-Chaumont, and a good number

Parc André-Citroën.

Jardins du Ranelagh.

Trocadéro.

Square du Temple.

Parc de Belleville.

of simpler squares. However, the presidents of the Republic and the mayors of the capital were not to be outdone. They improved the greening of the city with major parks like Les Halles, La Villette, Bercy, and André-Citroën. The last two decades of the 20th century were particularly rich in landscaping efforts.

Most of these large parks are also audaciously-sized recreation fields. The slides at the Parc de Belleville have taken the place of the attraction park that gave Parisians their first roller-coaster thrills. The spurting fountains at the Parc André-Citroën and the dragon slide at La Villette are equally spectacular offerings.

Official gardens aside, Paris has thousands of small private gardens. Practically every street in Paris has some hidden private garden behind a carriage door or at the end of a long corridor. At the far end of long passageways in the 13th *arrondissement*, grapevines cover whole spans of walls. The Villas of Belleville and the Buttes-Chaumont have tiny "front yards," not to mention the gardens off limits to the public within certain venerable religious institutions. Though noisy and polluted, Paris is also a very green city.

Le Parc Monceau

In 1797, André-Jacques Garnerin, a soldier with a penchant for science, engaged in a particularly perilous exercise. He parachuted out of a hot air balloon and landed in the Parc Monceau. To be exact, he was in a basket suspended from a cone of fabric. The peaceful park has rarely seen such daring exploits.

The garden originally belonged to a small royal *château* (commissioned by the Orléans branch) in the tiny village of Mousseaux, then considered far from the heart of Paris. One of the owners was Philippe Égalité, Duke of Chartres and cousin of Louis XVI. After the French Revolution, Napoleon I gave the estate to his minister Cambacérès, but in 1852 Napoleon III decided to buy it back for the state. A section of the original park was sold off for an elegant residential development on the Monceau plain. Certain new residents of the neighborhood made sizable profits in the real estate speculation that accompanied city improvements conducted by Prefect Georges Eugène Haussmann. Other famed residents included kept ladies like the flaming redheaded beauty Valtesse de La Bigne. Her mansion inspired novelist Émile Zola for the home of *Nana*.

Engineer Jean-Charles Alphand transformed the remaining tract of land into a public park. The main entrance is through a lovely rotunda, formerly a tollhouse designed by Ledoux. Intriguing and diverse monuments were built or moved into the park, such as the arcade from the Paris City Hall after it was burned down during the Commune revolution, and a mysterious pyramid. Statues of Guy de Maupassant, Charles Gounod, Chopin, and Ambroise Paré stand round an oval pond, pompously named Naumachie in reference to Roman arenas, which were filled with water for mock naval battles. The ornate Corinthian column beside the pond reportedly came from the uncompleted mausoleum in Saint-Denis, commissioned by Catherine de' Medici for King Henri II.

Parc Monceau, a favorite playground for well-heeled children escorted by governesses, is a place out of time, inhabited by marble phantoms.

The colonnade bordering the Naumachie pool.

Rotunda, formerly a tollhouse,
at the park entrance.

ASSEMBLÉE NATIONALE

BRILLIE

1902-1905

MDCCCLXIV

The Sacré-Cœur Basilica in the night sky
with the Paris city hall in the foreground.

montmartre

The Sacré-Cœur basilica, atop the highest point on the Butte Montmartre.

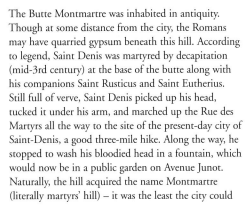

The Butte Montmartre was inhabited in antiquity. Though at some distance from the city, the Romans may have quarried gypsum beneath this hill. According to legend, Saint Denis was martyred by decapitation (mid-3rd century) at the base of the butte along with his companions Saint Rusticus and Saint Eutherius. Still full of verve, Saint Denis picked up his head, tucked it under his arm, and marched up the Rue des Martyrs all the way to the site of the present-day city of Saint-Denis, a good three-mile hike. Along the way, he stopped to wash his bloodied head in a fountain, which would now be in a public garden on Avenue Junot. Naturally, the hill acquired the name Montmartre (literally martyrs' hill) – it was the least the city could do for the three beheaded saints. Jesuit and Benedictine convents long shared the windy hillside with flour mills. High on the *butte*, the impressive alabaster-white Sacré-Cœur basilica has been place of prayer and a major pilgrimage for the faithful from the world over for a good century now.

However, it was hardly holiness that brought real international fame to the village of steep, narrow streets which often end as dizzying stairs. No, its fame is due to the artists and the party girls from Rue Lepic, Place des Abbesses, the Moulin de la Galette, and Place Blanche. In the 19th and 20th centuries, several generations of French cancan dancers and strip-tease artists wowed talented artists like Renoir, Picasso, Toulouse-Lautrec, and Utrillo. Every night was pure celebration.

The folklore has not completely faded away. Today's artists on Place du Tertre may not have the talent of Vincent Van Gogh who frequented the dance halls on Rue Lepic, and today's French cancan dancers may not have the spunk or sharp tongues of their ancestors "Grille d'Égout" ("Miss Gutter Grate") or "La Goulue" ("Miss Glutton"), but Montmartre will never, never, be an ordinary quarter. Its worn cobblestone lanes, its Lapin Agile cabaret, its Saint-Vincent cemetery, its long stairs leading to the Allée des Brouillards ("fog lane") will forever preserve a bit of the mystery of that Montmartre spirit.

Montmartre's vineyard.

Montmartre museum on Rue Cortot.

Saint-Pierre marketplace.

Restaurant
La Mère Catherine,
founded in 1793.

Allée des Brouillards.

Saint-Pierre-de-Montmartre
church.

Moulin Radet,
on Rue Lepic.

From left to right:
Saint-Jean-l'Évangéliste
church, place des Abbesses,
Rue des Saules,
and Villa des Arts.

Le Moulin de la Galette.

Place du Tertre.

From left to right:
Cité Véron, Villa Léandre,
and the stairs of Rue Foyatier.

111

SHOPS and SHOP SIGNS

For a long time, property developers had no qualms about scrapping outmoded interior décor in Parisian boutiques. Then one day, merchants began to realize that the undeniable charms of the old shops offered great possibilities. Nowadays, it is not at all unusual to see clothing shops proudly sporting old ceramic or wrought-iron signs from bakeries or butcher shops.

While old Paris boutiques do not necessarily qualify as historic sites, they are no longer being neglected. Quite a number of trustworthy old shops in Paris have never changed hands and continue to charm their clientele with their original décors dating back to the 1950s, or even much further: grocers, dressmakers, sewing shops, hardware shops…

Relaxing beside the lake.

Le Parc
Des Buttes-Chaumont

Charles Trenet's popular song *Un Jardin extraordinaire* perfectly sums up the spirit of this extraordinary garden park in the northeastern working-class neighborhoods of Paris. It offers visitors a strange sensation of traveling through time and space.

The small Temple of Sibyl perched high on a cliff in the Parc des Buttes-Chaumont is a reproduction of the edifice in ruins in Tivoli, near Rome. Every single structure in the park is artificial. The cliffs and the *Aiguilles* (needles) that make up the artificial island in the lake were inspired by those near the city of Étretat. The grotto with its concrete stalactites imitates sinkholes in southern France. In 1866, hills were built upon the rubble of the vast city dumps. Caverns were carved out of abandoned gypsum quarries.

The park's landscaping is exceptional indeed, one of the finest examples of Second Empire work. Much credit goes to Adolphe Alphand who also designed several other Paris parks and recreational areas.

With 25 hectares of hills and miniature forests, the park attracts sports enthusiasts, picnicking families, nature lovers, and wedding parties.

Tragic events occurred here during the Franco-German War of 1870. And during the *semaine sanglante*

(bloody week) of the Commune Revolution, the park was the battleground of French against French.

Those gory events are fairly forgotten today. Pretty ladies catch summer rays on the sloping lawns. Children play hide-and-seek and pretend to be afraid in the partially covered 200 steps cutting in and out of the island's needles. Lovers make believe they are alone in the world within the circular Temple of Sybil and far above all of Paris.

Hundred-year-old trees
in the park.

Bottom:
The Temple of Sybil.

Park entrance pavilion.

Le Pont des Suicidés
(Suicide bridge).

Molière and La Fontaine (25th division).

Oscar Wilde (89th division).

PÈRE-LACHAISE CEMETERY

Allan Kardec (44th division).

Simone Signoret and Yves Montand (44th division).

Jim Morrison (6th division).

In 1803, Prefect Frochot, a politician who, like many sovereigns left their mark on the geography of Paris, decided to make a cemetery of land that had once belonged to Father La Chaize, lifelong confessor to King Louis XIV. The project was assigned to architect Brongniart, better known for his design of the Bourse de Paris (stock market).

The new necropolis was no immediate success, as families held staunchly to their burial traditions in neighborhood churchyards. City officials cleverly decided to "launch" the Père-Lachaise cemetery by bringing in the revered relics of medieval lovers Héloïse and Abélard. Next, the remains of Molière and La Fontaine were transferred to the cemetery. The funerary marketing plan had the desired effect. Celebrities made the cemetery attractive. Even characters in popular novels, such as certain heroes in Honoré de Balzac's *Comédie Humaine*, wished to be buried at Père-Lachaise.

A stroll through the winding and steep paths at Père-Lachaise cemetery is a voyage through literary, political, and art history. Colette's tomb seems to stand guard over the eternal slumber of a noble assembly: marshals of the Empire, Murat, Ney and Masséna, actresses Sarah Bernhardt and Simone Signoret, dancer Isadora Duncan, Balzac and Gérard de Nerval, along with Alfred de Musset and Chopin.

The tombs at Père-Lachaise Cemetery have inspired occult practices and rites of veneration of all sorts. The dolmen dedicated to Allan Kardec attracts spiritualists from the world over. The Mur des Fédérés is a memorial to the Communards shot here. The sphinx upon the tomb of Oscar Wilde has seen countless pilgrimages of gays paying their respects. Bur for the last thirty years, Jim Morrison's grave has drawn the largest crowds of all.

Cité des Fleurs, 17th arrondissement.

Rue de Pomereu, 16th arrondissement.

Rue Santos-Dumont, 15th arrondissement.

La Campagne à Paris, 20th arrondissement.

Cité Florale, 13th arrondissement.

PARIS VILLAGE LIFE

La Ruche (literally, "the beehive"),
Passage de Dantzig, 15th arrondissement.

Saint-Germain-de-Charonne church
on Rue de Bagnolet, 20th arrondissement.

Hameau Boileau, 16th arrondissement.

Rue des Fêtes, 20th arrondissement.

Cité Verte, 13th arrondissement.

The twenty *arrondissements* of Paris are divided into four quarters, making a total of eighty quarters. But how many actually contain villages? Real Paris-style villages with houses along narrow winding streets, steeped in history, date back to before the capital's several expansion programs.

The Saint-Germain-de-Charonne church and its tiny cemetery stand beside an old village square, just a stone's throw from the towers of the Saint-Blaise quarter.

Near the bustling Porte de Bagnolet, several dozen houses make up the neighborhood called La Campagne à Paris (literally, "the country in Paris"). This former working-class quarter is now considered a gem, as is the Mouzaïa area with its cozy townhouses located in the shadow of the towers of the Place des Fêtes. In lanes bearing the names of former presidents of the French Republic you may cross the path of one of the city's rare beekeepers with honey-producing hives. Similarly, there will always be a resident of the 13th *arrondissement* bragging about being a wine producer (in good years) with just a single vine of grapes tucked away in a private lane.

Charming "villas" in the 14th and 15th arrondissements have always attracted artists. A certain number of artists have moved into La Ruche, a bizarre tower in the middle of an enclosed garden.

The Cité des Fleurs in the 17th *arrondissement* (between Avenue de Clichy and Rue de la Jonquière) is famed for its chestnut trees, while the well-known Rue Saint-Vincent in Montmartre will forever retain its village charm.

Passage Denfert,
14th arrondissement.

Rue de Meaux, 19th arrondissement.

Cité Varenne, 19th arrondissement.

Square Vergennes, 15th arrondissement.

Cité Fleurie, 13th arrondissement.

Rue Berton,
16th arrondissement.

Le Parc Montsouris

The 1878 ribbon-cutting ceremony for this park was marred by a tragic event. All the water suddenly drained out of the park's artificial lake as if someone had simply pulled the plug out of an ordinary bathtub. Legend has it that the engineer in charge of the park's waterworks was so distraught he committed suicide. True or not, it was not the only tragic event in the peaceful park's history. In 1991, a raging fire consumed the Bardo, which was originally built on the Champ-de-Mars for the 1867 Universal Exhibition as Tunisia's pavilion, a small-scale model of the palace belonging to the Bey of Tunis. After the Exhibition closed, it was moved to the highest point in the park. Today, the park's belvedere is gone forever.

Despite the tragic stories, the park is one of the most tranquil places in all Paris. This pendant on the southern collar of Paris is much like its northern sister the Parc des Buttes-Chaumont offering numerous recesses, glades, lawns, and shaded benches where you can hide away and forget the city.

At the outset of the 20th century, artists the world over came to live in the neighborhood adjacent to this park noted for its rolling hills. Writers Henry Miller and Anaïs Nin lived out their passionate love affair in a home located at 18 bis, villa Seurat. The tiny cul-de-sac (a private alley today) also owes its international fame to artists like Lurçat, Soutine, and Dali. The very elegant Nicolas de Staël lived at 7, rue Gauguet, while the painting couple Hans Hartung and Anna Eva Bergman moved in next door at number 5 of the same street. Amédée Ozenfant was fortunate enough to rent the villa at 53, avenue Reille, one of the first projects of the young architect Le Corbusier.

PARIS CAFÉS

Les Deux Magots, Le Café Flore, and La Closerie des Lilas are monuments in their own right. No Hollywood movie filmed in Paris ever passes up filming the terraces of these typically Parisian settings. Life in Paris runs on the cafés' schedules.

There are really two types of cafés. There are the big names, often veritable historic monuments, like the Café Procope on Rue de l'Ancienne-Comédie, founded in 1672 by young Sicilian Francesco Procopio dei Coltelli. Intellectual and literary trends were set at the cafés near the Saint-Germain-des-Prés church or on Boulevard du Montparnasse. Having a fashionable artist or writer as a regular patron was enough to draw crowds. This phenomenon is still at work, and explains the popularity of the new "in" places between Bastille and Belleville with their décors imitating bistros of bygone days. However most Paris cafés are neither trendy, historic, nor esthetic. No Nobel Literary Prize winners in their clientele, just neighborhood regulars who come for drinks and something simple to eat. Most want an expresso (affectionately called "le petit noir") with maybe a small glass of water which barmen still occasionally call "Château Chirac", or a glass of beer ("une pression"), or an anise-based drink ("un Ricard" or "un 51"), or drinks flavored with diverse syrups ("Tomate", "Perroquet", or "Mauresque"), or the Suze-cassis cocktail (not to be confused with the Suez Canal, although one too many might make you Red Sea or even see red). Not exactly chic, but nothing could be more typically Parisian.

Opéra-Bastille.

La Bastille

Precious little remains of the fortress-prison La Bastille, symbol of absolutism and arbitrary judgment. Today, only vestiges of its foundations jut out onto a platform in the Bastille metro station, and like chalk marks around a murder victim's body, a few white lines sketch the contours of the most famous (yet non-existent) monument of the history of France.

The storming of the Bastille occurred on July 14, 1789. In the days that followed, the prison was completely razed. Stone by stone, the prison that once made Parisians shudder was dismantled in the space of a few months. An enterprising fellow picked up the debris and sold off pieces to buyers in far-flung corners of France.

The prison may not have been as formidable as then commonly believed. Only a handful of privileged nobles and writers were locked up there, including a great number of 18th-century libertine authors.

Passions reached a feverish pitch when the new Opéra-Bastille opened to the public in 1989. However, there were no raging crowds intent on destroying it, though some people would still be very happy to see it torn down. Of all the major 20th-century projects, the new opera house has been the most virulently criticized. Nevertheless, music lovers appreciate it. Concerts are constantly sold out. Verdi, Puccini, and Mozart now have an auditorium on the scale of their grandeur.

The new opera house has certainly altered the ambiance of the Place de la Bastille. Droves of revelers are back, just like in the heyday of the famous dance hall Le Balajo favored by dancers from all over France. New bars, modern cafés, and flashy discotheques sprang up on Rue de Lappe, Rue de Charonne, Rue de la Roquette. The Bastille area of the 1990s quickly became one of the hippest areas in the city. Beside the Opéra-Bastille, beneath the flashing neon signs lighting up side streets, the memory of the terrifying fortress has withered away, and Paris night owls have found a new haven.

Café on Rue de Lappe.

Opposite: the Colonne de Juillet
in the center of Place de la Bastille.

Café La Palette
on Avenue Ledru-Rollin.

Workshops on Rue Titon.

The Faubourg Saint-Antoine area has many such courtyards designed for artisans' shops and living quarters.

FAUBOURG SAINT-ANTOINE

At one time or another, every courtyard and every alleyway in the labyrinth of the Faubourg Saint-Antoine quarter has had its cabinetmaker, woodworker, or upholsterer's workshop. From Place de la Bastille to Rue de Montreuil, an entire section of Paris long made its living almost exclusively in furniture and interior decoration for homes throughout the capital. Many of the artisans were veritable artists. Like most Paris neighborhoods, the Faubourg Saint-Antoine now has fewer artisans. But it is still packed with furniture shops.

The major revolts of the 19th century took place in the streets of this district – uprisings that toppled monarchs and emperors. Restless residents frequently threw up barricades to block the narrow entrance to the Faubourg. It was on one such barricade that lawmaker Jean-Baptiste Baudin was killed. Baudin was one of the few opponents of the December 1851 coup d'état that transformed the Second Republic into the Second Empire. It is still a boisterous street, but nowadays the Rue du Faubourg Saint-Antoine rumbles with the rally cries of demonstrators, techno-music parades, and Gay Pride parades marching from Bastille to Place de la Nation.

Although there are fewer artisans than before, and although fashion designers and posh restaurants have moved into the area, the Faubourg Saint-Antoine remains a working-class district, especially around the Marché d'Aligre. This colorful and very lively marketplace attracts shoppers from far and wide with both inexpensive food and gourmet delights.

Le Barrio Latino, 46, rue du Faubourg Saint-Antoine,
12th arrondissement.

Paris
Night Life

The girls at the Lido, the French cancan dancers at
the Moulin Rouge, and the striptease artists at Pigalle are
not the only queens of Paris night life. Every evening
after sundown, thousands of festivities are being prepared
in every quarter of the city. Every quarter has a few
streets, a few bars, a few special venues where night life
in Paris is vibrant, to say the least!

With the first grand dance halls like Le Bal Mabille
on Avenue Montaigne, or La Closerie des Lilas, and
Saint-Germain-des-Prés nightclubs like Le Tabou and
Le Lorientais, Paris has never slumbered. In the early years
of the 20th century, crowned heads from the world over
would flock from one Paris night spot to another in what
became known as "la tournée des grands ducs" (a more
refined term for "bar hopping"). Among the revelers were
real dukes and a few royal highnesses. Champagne flowed
at Maxim's, as well as at chic cozy lounges and bordellos
like Le Chabanais and the One-Two-Two.

The working classes were not to be outdone. They
whooped it up at the *guinguettes* on the outskirts of Paris
where wine was cheaper.

When the first discotheques appeared in the 1960s,
Paris jetted into a new era. The new "in" places were
Chez Régine, Chez Castel, then later Les Bains
Douches, Le Palace, and Le Queen. At the dawn of the
21st century, Paris night life has made a place for itself
on Rue Oberkampf, in Ménilmontant, along the banks
of the Seine and the Canal Saint-Martin, around the
Bastille and Rue de Charonne. But the ever-popular
areas of the Champs-Élysées, Montparnasse, and the
Latin Quarter have not been left in the dust. They are
as happening as ever.

131

La Bibliothèque nationale de France
Site François-Mitterrand

The four towers of the new national library represent four open books. They announce the renovation of Paris' eastern Left Bank.

Le Batofar, café-barge.

Four open books, or rather four glass towers framing a sunken garden make up the new national library beside the River Seine in eastern Paris. President François Mitterrand's project has now become part of the Paris cityscape and centerpiece of the mammoth Left Bank development project, a neighborhood unlike any other. While the library has been completed, construction of the new quarter continues upon a vast platform covering portions of the Gare d'Austerlitz railway tracks. The plan to build a new national library to replace the aging library on Rue Vivienne dates back to 1989. The project presented by architect Dominique Perrault created quite a stir. Years of searing debate followed on what the edifice should or should not be. Some people predicted the books in the glass towers "would be roasted" by the sunlight. Many warned that the elderly might slip and fall on rain-slick steps leading up to the esplanade. Others howled about the central garden being off limits to the general public. Pessimists trumpeted that the library computer system would never work. The gloomiest of these predictions actually did come true. Nevertheless, this prestigious building has had a positive effect on the surrounding area. A brand new Parisian neighborhood has sprung to life. Shops, cafés, and restaurants have moved in, too. Art galleries have set up in nearby streets. The new riverside Arthur-Rimbaud walkway attracts strolling pedestrians and offers views and access to a peaceful fleet of river craft moored at the quays. Every evening, throngs of Parisians flock to these floating cafés, restaurants, and showboats with amusing names like Le Batofar and La Guinguette Pirate. The rehabilitation of this previously rundown section of eastern Paris is well underway.

Water levels rise and fall more than 80 feet (25 meters) in the canal's locks.

HOTEL DU NORD

HOTEL DU NORD

CAFÉ RESTAURANT

Le canal Saint-Martin

"Atmosphère, atmosphère, est-ce que j'ai une gueule d'atmosphère ?" ("Ambiance? D'you think with a mug like mine I'd want ambiance!") This famous line was spoken by the throaty actress Arletty in Marcel Carné's 1938 film *L'Hôtel du Nord*. That one line immortalized the charming footbridges over Saint-Martin Canal, undoubtedly one of the most popular and most typically Parisian features of the capital.

The canal is a favorite site for strolls on the quays, fishing, and watching lazy barges float by. For roughly 3 miles (4.8 km), shady plane trees, locks, and bridges give the canal that rather special *atmosphère*.

Napoleon I was behind the enormous project designed firstly to alleviate congested river traffic on the Seine, secondly to shorten barges' trips by connecting the river with the Canal de L'Ourcq (opened in 1808), and thirdly, to improve Paris' water supply. Digging did not really begin until 1822, but the Saint-Martin canal quickly became a thriving industrial zone because of the advantages of being supplied by barge. Paper mills, tanneries, and porcelain manufacturers quickly moved in. Napoleon III deemed it best to cover the stretch of the canal from the Bastille to the Rue du Faubourg-du-Temple to facilitate traffic, including the movement of

troops sent to "pacify" the working-class neighborhoods in eastern Paris. The canal went underground. Occasional skylights make the tunnel's water a little less gloomy. In the early 1960s, certain city officials toyed with the idea of filling in the canal for an expressway through the heart of eastern Paris. Thankfully, that project was scrapped. The canal still has its special ambiance, but now the young, hip, "in" crowd of Paris is flocking to smart cafés and posh restaurants along the quays. Business has switched to the likes of fashion houses, website design firms, art galleries, art studios, movie theaters, and film production companies.

Bernard Tschumi's bright red follies pop up here and there in the gardens of La Villette.

The Canal de l'Ourcq flows past the Géode and the Cité des Sciences.

The *Argonaute* submarine.

Today, the enormous cheerful park is thronged by children, Sunday soccer players, and music lovers. But it used to bear the gory nickname "la cité du sang" (Bloodville). For over a century, from 1867 to 1974, La Villette was home to one of Europe's largest slaughterhouses. La Grande Halle, perfectly in tact today, was the beef market, and its smaller sister building was the sheep market. In its heyday, La Villette employed about 3,000 people. Bankruptcy and the closing of the slaughterhouses brought the opportunity to transform the vast perimeter into a museum dedicated to science. Fighter aircraft, optical games, and hundred of exhibits now unveil the mysteries of science and technology. All around the museum, the old slaughterhouses were getting facelifts as new buildings sprang up. The park features a collection of the most astounding monuments erected at the close of the 20th century. The Geode, a stainless steel sphere, is actually a hemispheric screen offering breathtaking movie screenings. The Zénith is home to the largest rock and roll concert hall in Paris.

The Cité de la Musique is home to the Conservatoire national (the national music conservatory), the Musée de la Musique (the museum of musical instruments), and a concert hall. Audiences are greeted by bright red cubical "follies" popping up out of the park grounds, charming buildings designed by architect Bernard Tschumi. A dozen theme gardens with scents and varying landscapes, an extraordinary slide in the shape of a dragon, and numerous other attractions make La Villette a place with something for everyone.

La Grande Halle, once the center of Paris' livestock trade.

Flea markets

The flea markets of Paris sprang to life upon the old ramparts that surrounded the city. The fortress walls were glaringly ineffective even before they were completed. The technology of warfare had outpaced them. But the fortifications became the rendezvous of the social outcasts. Rag-and-bone men began trading in the ditches around the walls. Makeshift markets sprang up in the 1920s on the demolished military installations. Today, the flea markets draw millions of visitors annually. Each of the three Paris flea markets has its own ambiance and clientele. While the Porte de Vannes flea market seems to be the poor sister of the others in terms of choice and popularity, bargain hunters will always find something to satisfy their hearts' desire. The Porte de Montreuil flea market draws a more popular crowd. Stalls are simply set up on a parking lot near the ringroad expressway.

The Saint-Ouen flea market is a labyrinth, a veritable city within a city, a seemingly unending stretch of tiny neighborhoods. Each market has its specialty and the ambiance changes noticeably from one section to the next. So much choice makes heads spin. Clothes and costume jewelry at the Marché Malik, founded (according to legend) by a Yugoslavian prince. Art Deco items at the Marché des Rosiers; Napoleon III style at the Marché Biron. Or how about the wonderfully messy open displays of unloaded merchandise on Rue des Rosiers and under the bridges of the ringroad expressway? In any case, all this shopping and walking will call for a stop at Chez Louisette. This amazing restaurant with its bric-a-brac decoration offers a nearly permanent flow of buskers ("so typically Parisian!") to serenade you as an accordionist accompanies them in their repertoires of Edith Piaf songs.

THE NEW STADIUM: LE STADE DE FRANCE

One evening in July 1998, the Stade de France in Saint-Denis entered the annals of history, when les Bleus (the "Blues") took the World Soccer Cup. The freshly constructed monumental stadium had barely taken its place in the urban landscape. For years, the capital area had been sorely lacking an appropriately sized stadium. The 1924 Olympic Games trials were held at the stadium in Colombes, hardly worthy of such an event. When France was selected to host the 1992 World Soccer Cup, the thorny issue of selecting a site for a new stadium pitted the ultra-modern city of Évry against Saint-Denis. The latter won as it offered the advantage of greater proximity to Paris. The enormous stadium, christened Stade de France only months before the game, is particularly well-equipped with easy direct public transportation.

The winning teams in the competition for design of the stadium were two firms of architects Macary & Zubléna, and Regembal & Costantini. They gave France a truly remarkable stadium. It covers nearly 15 acres, roughly the equivalent of Place de la Concorde. The bleachers are completely mobile, making this the world's largest adjustable Olympic stadium. The 13,000-ton halo-shaped roof sits on eighteen tapered steel needles, and thus seems to float in midair, 141 feet off the ground, light as a feather. Since 1998, the stadium has hosted dozens of major events, from rock concerts to rugby matches, drawing hundreds of thousands of spectators to fill the grand stands of this already legendary structure. Few monuments can boast offering their contemporaries so many unforgettable memories in so few years of operation.

Château de Bagatelle and its half-moon front.

Canoeing on the lake.

Entrance to the Château de Bagatelle.

Rose garden at Bagatelle.

Square des Poètes.

Le Pré-Catelan.

In the 19th century, fashionable ladies would take daily carriage rides through Paris' western woods, going down the paths as slowly as possible so that bystanders could better admire their magnificent gowns. The pathways were initially traced under King Louis XIV for his hunting parties. However, it was under Emperor Napoleon III, an aficionado of gardens, that the former primeval forest of Rouvray was transformed into a large public park with natural English-style landscaping and became the Bois de Boulogne. As park engineers "tamed" Nature, they enhanced the park with *le lac supérieur* (the upper lake) and *le lac inférieur* (the lower lake). Wishing to admire the grace and beauty of his newly created park,

the Emperor commissioned architect Gabriel Davioud to design the imperial kiosk, a building inspired by Swiss chalets and placed on the lower lake's northern island. In 1855, the Longchamp racetrack, the *hippodrome*, was laid out on grounds where a small medieval château and an abbey once stood.

Every year until World War I, on France's national holiday, an impressive military parade was held at the Longchamp hippodrome.

Nothing remains in these woods of the residences built by the aristocracy, save the Château de Bagatelle, a prime example of the "follies," lovers' rendezvous built by gallant nobles of Louis XV's time. What we see today is the

19th-century renovation of Bagatelle. It belonged to Parisian socialite Lord Hertford and his adoptive son Richard Wallace, the inventor and donor of the famous green fountains, which still grace the city. Today, Bagatelle is best known for its splendid botanical gardens.

Among the other treasures tucked away in the Bois de Boulogne are some fabulous settings for a stroll through time. Children can step right into a 19th-century storybook world at the Jardin d'Acclimatation, a small zoological garden with delightful old-fashioned playground equipment. Beside the famous Pré-Catelan restaurant, a charming Shakespeare garden evokes several plays by the great English playwright.

Le château
de versailles

Leto and her children, Apollo and Diane,
sculpture by the Marsy brothers.

Louis XIV, the Sun King, set the most brilliant minds in orbit about him to design and occupy what was to be the most spectacular accomplishment of his reign: the Château and domain of Versailles. The King hardly liked the capital and often felt personally endangered by the revolts of the Fronde (an eight-year civil war). After the death of Cardinal Mazarin in 1661, his reign truly began. One of his first acts was to enlarge his father's (Louis XIII) small hunting lodge palace. The modernization effort spanned twenty years. After the renovation of the "old palace" came the construction of the colossal "new palace." Architect Louis Le Vau quickly departed from the influence of the initial castle and laid plans for a vast modern palace with elegant stone façades crowned with balustrades and a flat roof of Italian inspiration. Meanwhile, landscape architect Le Nôtre was designing gardens, rectilinear pathways, groves, canals, and ponds.

The pace of the work stepped up when the Sun King announced in 1678 his firm intention to make Versailles his official residence. The famous garden-side Hall of Mirrors then went up to mask permanently the façade of the old palace. Hardouin-Mansart and Robert de Cotte built the magnificent Royal Chapel, and the Orangeries were erected in the park. Versailles had become the center of the kingdom. All of France's grandees, lords and artists, took up residence in the Château de Versailles. Molière and Lully gave the best of their talents while the Sun King ruled over hundreds of nobles whose lives centered around regal feasts, the rigors of exacting court etiquette, and boredom – the only cure for which was scheming and plotting.

Bassin de Flore, a.k.a. *Spring*, by Tuby.

Opposite:
Venus, by Coysevox.

Petit Trianon.

OPÉRA
TROCADERO
BASTILLE
LOUVRE
ST-MICHEL
NOTRE-DAME
CHAMPS-ÉLYSÉES
METRO
BLAUPUNKT
AUTORADIO
Black Cat
BANANIA
CHOCOLAT MENIER
TITANIC
SOUTHERN PACIFIC LINES
Président
Bridel
NOTRE-DAME DE PARIS
PLACE SAINT-GERMAIN DES PRES
HARLEY-DA
CALIFORNIA US 66
ARIZONA US 66
NEW MEXICO US 66
TEXAS US 66
America's Main Street

Our thanks to:

Angelo Tota and the staff of Leyre Photogravure (14th arrondissement)

Mme Catherine Le Teuff, from the Centre Georges-Pompidou (4th arrondissement)

Jacques Lebar extends his special thanks to:

Jean Caraux

Silvia Ficai and Stefan Matecki

Jean-Marie Crestia, Jean-François Crestia and Christophe Boulot at Brasserie La Maison, (17th arrondissement),

The staff and management of La Tour d'Argent restaurant,

The staff and management of Lucas Carton restaurant,

Mme Galichet, Hôtel Au Manoir Saint-Germain (6th arrondissement).

Mme Brigitte Agneray, Hôtel Novotel Les Halles (1th arrondissement)

Marie-Odile Orfila and M. Hollard, passage Lhomme (11th arrondissement), for their warm welcome

M. G. Chudzinski and M. Genest, Optimege for their valuable help on the Champs-Élysées (8th arrondissement)

Le Barrio Latino, 46, rue du Faubourg-Saint-Antoine (12th arrondissement)

The staff and management of Central Color labotary (16th arrondissement), particulary departement E6

Isabelle Chemin, art director, for her precious collaboration

The entire staff of Parigramme and above all François Besse

Conception et réalisation graphique : Isabelle Chemin

Photogravure Leyre, à Paris

Achevé d'imprimer en janvier 2007
sur les presses de l'imprimerie Mame, à Tours (France)

Dépôt légal : janvier 2003

ISBN : 978-2-84096-267-5